2.8 to 4.5 ...
Assembly Required

A Blueprint to Building a Positive Workplace Culture

Keith W. Lazar

ISBN: 978-1-4834-7638-4 (sc)
ISBN: 978-1-4834-7637-7 (e)

Library of Congress Control Number: 2017916719

Lulu Publishing Services rev. date: 10/28/2017

CONTENTS

ACKNOWLEDGEMENTS

I want to give a huge thank you to an awesome staff. They embraced new philosophies for the greater good. We had fun and accomplished much together. I will say this about them, which I believe to be the highest compliment. If I were to start a competing company, I would certainly approach them first to invite them to join me in the venture. I am confident that most would seriously consider the opportunity and make a short-term sacrifice in spite of the risk.

A great appreciation goes to the board of directors who were patient and understood our road to achievement, even when the staff expressed apprehension in my leadership style at the beginning of my tenure. Skepticism was expected because I was new. The approach to redirect the organization was diametrically opposite to which they had become accustomed. Again I heard, "that is not the way we have always done it,". It fueled doubt and uncertainty.

A special note of appreciation and acknowledgement goes to Rachel, the board chair. She encouraged this compilation of experiences and lessons learned.

A special thank you goes to all my past associates. I would like to name everyone who has been a part of my journey, but I fear omitting someone. However, I would like to recognize a few individuals who worked with me for separate companies. They played key roles in the first step of the culture-enhancement process of each organization.

The first person I want to acknowledge is Arlene. I first met her and her husband, Kevin, during an annual operation review of their business. Both were very positive and created strong first impressions.

Our operation needed to expand our staff so I reached out to Arlene. I assumed I could teach her the basics about our business and I knew she would be successful because of her great interpersonal skills. She accepted the challenge and began her journey down a career path in the financial services industry in which she has limited or no experience. I was confident that she would embrace the basics and in doing so would set a great example for the staff. In a short time, I noticed her colleagues reaching out to her for guidance. Today Arlene is an officer and board member of that company, a great achievement of which she and her family should take pride. Unfortunately, I accepted an offer from another company (financial institution) and was not able to fully enjoy her contribution to the enhancement of the company culture.

The second person I want to recognize is Kim, my first significant hire in the institution about which this guide was written on the journey from 2.8 to 4.5. I remember my first impression of her in the interview process. She was working for a retailer and, like Arlene, had no experience in our industry. However, she was professional, had a positive attitude, and very good interpersonal skills. I believed she was someone who could learn the industry and set a good example as she progressed in the company. Today she is an officer and plays a vital role on the management team. Her organizational skills are incredible as she basically does the work of three people. The staff, no matter what capacity, frequently reaches out to her for guidance and leadership. I am proud of how she has developed as a leader and a speaker. I really enjoyed observing her personal and professional growth.

I hope that someday the opportunity would present itself for Arlene and Kim to meet. That would be a thrill as they both possessed a strong work ethic and other key elements of effective leadership. They are true examples of how one can transcend expectations, grow, and lead.

I also need to spotlight Dawn and Debbie who made amazing promotions to officer status. They were always, positive, practical, professional, and possessed great interpersonal skills. They were always willing to share their ideas and thoughts. They too had limited or no experience in our financial services industry. I trusted them immensely. They set a good example of how a positive attitude can propel one to success.

One amazing member of the staff to also be acknowledged was Margaret. She was very well organized and had anything and everything imaginable at her workstation. I always tried to stump her with some unusual office-supply request. I could never do it. Not only did she always have what I needed, but she knew exactly where it was. She and her husband Dan always volunteered to assist the company in any public service function. Every organization should have a Margaret. She could perform almost any company task and will be missed when she retires.

These individuals and many more who I have declined to name for fear of omission were the ones who made the enhancement of the company from 2.8 to 4.5. I salute them as they have my greatest admiration.

I dedicate this book to my family and especially my wife, who kept me grounded when my ego started to inflate. Because of their encouragement, I learned that I can always do better and I should never rest on my past accomplishments, for the rear view mirror is small and the windshield is large.

I have been blessed with two great children. They and their families are a true joy to be near. I love to observe how they have prospered and are now growing their children. They are my true legacy.

INTRODUCTION

A business has three primary objectives:

1. To be the first choice by consumers for the product and/or service that is offered
2. To be the investment of choice by those who own or have the ability to buy stock in the company
3. To be the employer of choice in the market

Accomplishing the first two objectives becomes extremely difficult if you are not the employer of choice in your market. Therefore, to be the employer of choice, your business must provide a workplace culture that others seek and envy.

Since retiring, I have been asked to write about my experience on how to grow the culture in an organization. The concept has a broad range of applications, including making a department, a work area, a branch, or even *you* the best that can be. My goal is to provide a guide to enhancement for everyone, from frontline supervisor all the way to the CEO and even those who aspire to be promoted to leadership positions.

If your associates or don't enjoy working for the company, then their attitudes will be tainted, and they will be unable to achieve their full personal potential and even that of the company. By the way, I always intentionally avoid referring to the staff as employees. Instead, I have chosen to use the words associates, staff, or colleagues. This promotes the concept of teamwork as compared to the assumption that the definition of employee is one who is used.

If one cannot achieve their potential and feel fulfilled in their job, then this will domino into mediocre customer care and service. The company—including the staff area, department, or branch—will be unable to achieve its goals and objectives and exceed the great service desired by its customers and expected by the company. A happy staff means happy customers, resulting in loyal customers. Loyal customers influence referrals, resulting in great sales. Great sales result in great growth, great opportunities, and great profits.

Many companies assert that the customer is number one and the main focal point of the organization. I believe that your staff is number one. If the staff members believe that the company is truly dedicated to their well-being and feel their importance, then this feeling will transfer to the customers. Their appreciation—combined with other concepts noted in this publication—will achieve greater results.

I derived part of the title, "2.8 to 4.5," from the results of an internal staff survey consisting of thirty-five questions, the first part of strategic planning. If your company does not have a positive culture, then the strategic plan objectives will become more difficult to achieve. The exercise assists management in determining the company's cultural status.

I will focus on the first question, which I believe to be the most important of the survey: "On a scale of 1 to 5, with 5 being the best, how would you rate your satisfaction with working here?" Respondents were asked to anonymously complete the questionnaire and return it via mail to an independent consultant, who then tabulated and shared the results with the board of directors, the president/CEO, and the management team. I did not participate in the survey.

The board of directors selected a consultant to have the survey performed only after I had been with the organization a very short time yet long enough to get to know the staff and how the organization functioned. The first question had a composite score of 2.8 out of a possible 5.0. This was not the best result but did establish a baseline by which progress could be measured.

Twenty years later, the same question was asked with the result of 4.5 out of a possible 5.0. So why such a dramatic change? This guide identifies the challenges, failures, strategies, and successes on our road to 4.5.

The second part of the title, "Assembly Required," implies that you must build your culture piece by piece. By comparison, think about the last time you assembled a model airplane, a bicycle, a piece of furniture, a jigsaw puzzle, or something as complex as a home theater system. Where do you begin, and what would you do without instructions? In the business environment, you are expected to build a positive culture without a guide. Developing a positive workplace culture is significantly more important than building a model airplane, although there is a parallel of concepts.

In my younger years, I loved to put together model airplanes. I would open the box and take out the parts, looking for the easiest and largest parts to assemble. I checked the step-by-step instructions and made sure I had all the parts and, most importantly, the glue. Sometimes I tried to assemble the parts without the instructions. When I tried this, the project just did not turn out to resemble the picture on the box. It was sloppy-looking, and I had leftover parts. The most difficult aspect about the assembly was patiently waiting for some glued parts to dry before I could move forward.

I want to repeat what I just said: the most difficult aspect of the assembly was patiently waiting for some glued parts to dry. Sometimes the process was made more complicated when I used too much glue and smeared the excess on my fingers. My fingers became sticky, and it became an obstacle to the next delicate parts connection. In time, as the construction manager, I completed the model. The final step was placing the decals. I learned that without patience, the model looked a little sloppy. However, when I was willing to endure, used the instructions as my guide, and remained diligent, then the model looked professionally done. I then would sit back and enjoy the creation.

I can draw another parallel with a jigsaw puzzle. What do you do first? You study the picture, open the box, and sort the pieces. Your first strategy is to sort the frame from the pieces. From the frame, you sort out the four corners, which support the frame, which provides a foundation for the other pieces. The same goes for your company or department. Who are the corners that support the frame? Who are the parts of the frame that provide a foundation for the other pieces? Over time and with much patience, piece by piece, you build a picture that becomes your proud creation. Only then can you sit back and enjoy your hard work.

The same can be said for building an exemplary culture. Maybe before you start the process, you should go buy a model airplane, a model car, or even a jigsaw puzzle. Test your patience, but don't open the box until you have read these recommendations on how to build a strong culture. With each step—and I mean every step—think about the parallel to building culture. Once complete, you might think about displaying your creation in your office or workstation as a reminder of what it takes to build a strong culture.

Are you the glue, or are you the project manager? You might be both. Make sure you have all the parts. Review the instructions. Place them in the right places. Let the journey begin.

The biggest challenge you will encounter with a company conversion will be making changes in staff attitude. Many longtime staff will probably be set in their ways and have minimal experience understanding the concept of a team. They will be slow to realize that their territorial attitude will be hurting their personal growth and not advancing the culture of the organization. They will be resistant to transformation. "This is the way we have always done it" might be their rationale for not accepting change.

Now, it may seem simple to merely change staff. However, what would you do if the key players were under contract and not employees at will? (This means that a contracted staff member must commit a significant breach to justify a personnel change.) Personnel change for the sake of change can be legally difficult. In addition, what would you do if many of the longtimers had a strong customer following? The consequences of personnel change would undoubtedly negatively impact the organization's reputation, erode customer confidence in the leadership, and ultimately result in a potential loss of business. In large communities or organizations, this may not be of concern. In smaller communities or organizations, this could result in extreme business sales setbacks.

So the question is, how do you improve the culture from a composite rating of 2.8 to 4.5? According to our consultant, the 4.5 was the best he had ever seen. During the enhancement of culture, the company achieved record growth, profitability, dividends, and a waiting list of those hoping to buy our privately held company minority stock at a price of more than two times book when the market price per share was more than twenty times the earnings per share. (Most analysts suggest you sell and not buy when the price is twice the book value or the price-earnings ratio is above twenty.) The company results were even more amazing when one considers that a staff number approximately two-thirds the national average efficiently ran the operation.

It should also be noted that 25 percent of the existing shareholders were on the waiting list to buy even more stock. The list was restricted to only those who were existing shareholders. Occasionally we would receive requests from non shareholders, but they were denied because they did not meet the criteria of ownership. However, some found existing shareholders who served as a straw man and had their name placed on the waiting list on their behalf. There was no restriction if an existing shareholder sold any of his or her shares to whomever he or she wanted. The waiting list was to serve as a source of liquidity for existing shareholders.

One final note of honor, after the 2010 financial crisis, an entity decided to interview businesses they determined were thriving before the economic crisis in 2008, continued to prosper during the period from 2008 to 2010, and then flourished thereafter. Businesses were categorized as either thriving or surviving. They concluded that ten states had no thriving businesses in our industry.

The agency requested to only interview one thriving business in our state, and the inquiry came to us. Their goal was to determine a correlation of success factors among thriving businesses. I met with a committee of three for an interview. They said they knew our numbers and ratios, but they wanted to know the other secrets to our success. I didn't think we had one. I soon discovered that we had a unique commonsense approach, which I will share in this publication. Our culture and the high quality staff was the secret to our success.

Another honor we received was our business being featured on the front page of a January 2 *Washington Post* edition. Eli Saslow, who later won a Pulitzer Prize for a different story, was traveling around the country doing features on all the communities in the nation with the same common name. He called me in advance and said he would like to meet just to discuss what was happening in our community.

He stopped by with a photographer and, of course, credentials. He shadowed me for a few days, including going home with me for lunch and out to dinner with my wife, our friends, and me. He even followed our staff to a community fund-raiser. He asked great questions and became enamored with our operation. He then wrote an article on our business.

I called my sister on the East Coast and told her she might want to go to the newsstand to buy a January 2, 2008 *Washington Post* edition. She called me back and said we were featured on the front page. This was a positive boost to our culture enhancement progression. I was very proud of the staff. In turn, they were proud of their business. It was a great endorsement on the road to enhancing company culture. Pride is a good thing.

To continue, I will discuss three areas on the road to 4.5:

1. The first area to evaluate is you, the title of chapter 1.
2. The second area, or chapter 2, pertains to your individual relationships with the staff.
3. The third area, chapter 3, is your relationship with the total organization or, in other words, the entire staff as a whole.

I have a final word before you begin your read. You will find certain thoughts or words of wisdom repeated throughout the chapters. They are worthy of noting.

CHAPTER 1

You

The first step in the process of elevating your culture begins with a self-evaluation. Who are you? Do you really want to be the best you can be? Are you committed to that dedication? What is your vision if you were designated to lead? What are your guiding principles? What are your values? Are you really meant to be a leader? Can you commit to change and flexibility? Can you set a good example? Are you patient? Are you a good communicator? Do you want a career or just a job?

A very high percentage of the staff in any organization is always looking for leadership. If you are a department head, district manager, vice president, CEO, crew foreman, or even someone aspiring to be such, your associates will typically be a reflection of you, your conduct, your appearance, how you treat people and solve problems, and more. Staff members tend to mirror their leader's values and attitudes. If you are not a leader, foreman, department head, or supervisor, then read this as if you were and use this as a guide to becoming one.

The lessons I have learned and my guiding principles follow. You need to know that I never aspired to be a CEO of a business in the industry where I ultimately found myself. Being in a leadership position for thirty-six of the forty-two years of my career was full of positive and negative experiences. I attempted to learn as much as possible from each. Even a negative experience can become positive.

My college major was business administration and economics. But I only selected that major because I was told that it might be the easiest. Choosing my major turned out to be a great asset in my career path. My biggest regret is not truly applying myself.

My road to fulfillment began with my very first job. My father was a company manager, and I needed money to help with personal and academic expenses. I lacked the self-confidence to apply anywhere else so I asked my dad if he would consider hiring me. He did not own the company, but he was the manager. I thought this might be a cushy job since I was his son. My dad agreed to hire me on three conditions:

1. I had to be the first to arrive at work every day.
2. I had to be the last to go home at night.
3. I had to accept and perform the dirtiest and worst jobs.

He explained that because I was the son of the manager, my fellow workers would constantly scrutinize me. They would be looking for favoritism. I learned that hard work and reliability was the first step to gaining respect from your peers. And yes, I made plenty of mistakes, but I just kept my mouth shut, learned from my experience, and moved forward.

I carried that philosophy throughout my career. I always wanted to be one of the first to arrive and the last to go home, and I would not be afraid to get my hands dirty. I would not request any staff member do something that I would not do myself. Many times I just went forward and did the job without requesting it be done by another. I aspired to set a good example. However, I did not desire to build complacency among the staff by having them adopt an expectation that I would always do their job.

Many nights and weekends, I would be found alone in my office. My goal was to be highly productive and be greatly organized or at least make it appear that way. Sometimes I would work evenings and weekends just to put my office in order and prioritize my calendar. I wanted customers and staff to see a clean, organized desk and office. First impressions are a key to leadership.

What does your workspace look like? Your organizational skills play a very important role in your efficiency and ultimately your productivity. Rarely will you find a member of any staff who admires his or her supervisor's messy, cluttered office. The first step in the process of culture enhancement is to set a good example.

After graduating from college, I returned to my hometown to again work for my dad's company. I had job offers from other companies but declined because the Vietnam War was ongoing and I had a low draft number. Our local Selective Service board estimated I would be called to duty in about three months. It would not be fair for another company to hire me and then be forced to fill my position because I was called to serve my country in the middle of training. I decided to await my fate.

Unknown to me, the war was winding down; therefore, the call for soldiers from our county was declining. In addition, many young men were enlisting, which reduced our monthly county draft quota. My wait was extended for a few more months until the war ceased and our forces began withdrawing from Vietnam.

Over time, the company sales manager took a chance and offered me a promotion to a territory salesman. My primary responsibility was to call on customers, explore their needs, and book anticipated seasonal products, which included the quantity and pricing. And then in most cases, I would actually deliver the product. I was still lacking self-confidence, but this experience immensely grew my ability to comfortably interact with people. I shied away from prospecting for new customers even though it was a requirement in my job description.

I have always asked myself about lessons learned from life experiences. To this point in time, I was learning the benefit of stepping outside my comfort zone. I was not the best at sales and again, as previously noted, lacked self-confidence. However, my reception by the customers was much better than I imagined. I'm guessing it was partly due to getting to know them as a deliverer of services and products in addition to being their sales contact. My self-confidence continued to grow.

I formed a couple philosophies from my experience. One was regarding sales. I am not a big proponent of sales quotas. I thus came to embrace a service culture, and here is how it happened.

The company always used a certain brand of pickup truck to deliver its products. When the trucks needed repair, they were sent to the dealership's service department. What was unusual was that the dealership owner also ran the service department. This was rare as most owners run the sales department and an experienced technician or mechanic usually runs the service department.

My employer was provided with great service. The dealership owner knew we relied heavily on our trucks to serve our customers in our busy season. It was essential to keep the trucks fully operational. So when it came time to buy new trucks, the company went nowhere else but to him. No other bids were ever obtained. Lesson learned: "If you give great service, then you will get great sales."

The dealership owner gave great service and reaped great sales. Therefore, I became an advocate of providing great service and not mandating the achievement of sales quotas. I became a true believer in a service, not sales, culture. I have seen how sales quotas result in unnecessary pressure on the staff and jealousy among associates. Sometimes customers are led to do something they really are unsure about. Trust becomes eroded, and customer service is compromised.

Another experience that benefited me greatly was when I attended a company-sponsored sales school. A presenter pointed out that in sales our goal is to probe the prospective customer in order to discover what this person may not like about another product, service, or company that he or she was using. We would then attempt to convince the prospect that we could cure that particular deficiency by using our company service or product.

He likened the concept of a visualization of the prospect wearing an arrow on the end of his or her nose. When the arrow is pointing upward, then the customer is satisfied. Our goal was to get the arrow turned sideways by exploiting the competitor's shortcomings and then bring it back to pointing upward when discussing our company.

I never extensively practiced this but instead used this concept as a means to greet customers. I discovered that if I would imagine an arrow on the nose of an existing or prospective customer, it would naturally make me smile. Now you need to understand that the customer does not know why I was smiling, but he or she liked it and felt I was being friendly and welcoming. Try it sometime. Use your imagination. I don't care who it is. You are guaranteed a smile in return.

I then decided that I needed to better leverage my college degree. I explored apprentice work as a management trainee with other companies throughout the Midwest. I began the interviewing and the application process.

Then my first big risk decision happened. I returned from an out-of-town company interview to a message from the president of a local company in a completely different industry. He wanted to talk to me. My dad asked me if maybe I were in trouble with that particular company. To my knowledge, I had no idea what the president and owner wanted.

The next day, I called for an appointment and then met with him. He offered me an entry-level job. I was making $10,000 per year at the time. He offered me $8,000. I accepted and went to work in a new industry. I felt that my opportunity for growth and advancement held more potential than my other choices. Again I took a risk and went outside my comfort zone. Ultimately I learned that sometimes you need to take a step backward before you can take two steps forward. It turned out to be a great move and was significant in my career.

I highly recommend that you daily reflect and ask yourself what lessons you have learned and what risks you have taken outside of your comfort zone. I continually appreciate that particular company president/owner for having faith in me, tolerating my mistakes, and continually challenging me to be better tomorrow than I was today. I frequently evaluated my daily experiences. It might be something

I did or said. I always challenged myself to be better with my next experience.

After joining the new company, I again found myself at the bottom of the barrel. I inherited the worst jobs, but I was still the first to arrive and the last to go home. However, it wasn't long before I was promoted and ultimately attained an officer position within six years. I was also fortunate to observe an absolutely brilliant president. I learned a great deal about the industry from him.

During those six years, a couple of key events happened in my life. The first and most important was my marriage and the beginning of a family. Again, it was an experience out of my comfort zone but yet with great anticipation. This gave me more stability in my life and a true sense of purpose. Marriage is great, and growing a family is very rewarding.

Our boy, Wes, later became the managing partner of a well-known business. I could not have asked for a better son. He is completely trustworthy and has awesome values. He married well and is currently raising a daughter to be successful. Our daughter is also incredible. She has an unbelievable job. Her high standards and values combined with a great work ethic, intelligence, and very personable attitude are the secrets to her success. She too married well, and with her husband, they are raising two young daughters the right way. Both of our children have embraced the importance of family.

Another key event in my professional growth was being exposed to a multiweek self-improvement course. I was fortunate that the company encouraged and paid for the opportunity. Again I thank that same president for the investment in me. However, it was up to me to apply the theory to everyday life experiences. About two dozen people were in the class, which met weekly for three hours over a multiweek period. Great friendships were made.

The very first philosophy I embraced was adopting the realization that true happiness does not come from what we do for ourselves. It actually comes from what we do for others. I thought to myself how fortunate I was to have a job that I could do just that and even get paid to do it. Wow!

I also started to develop a few ideals during this phase of my career as my self-confidence grew a bit more. Before I was promoted to a company officer, I worked alongside an older person who was a consummate complainer. I observed that her negativism became contagious. This person was well known in the community. I began sensing that her pessimism was influencing my attitude. However, the aforementioned self-improvement course was also influencing me. I worked with this individual professionally but learned to avoid her as much as possible. I began to develop an awareness of negativism as well as the benefits of having a positive attitude.

I decided to adopt another philosophy. It had to do with attitude. The self-improvement course taught me that the best way to develop a positive attitude is to practice enthusiasm. I embraced this concept and began practicing enthusiasm. I suggest that a good night's rest is a key component in the process. I have found that a positive attitude even helps you rebound in troubled times as well as effectively learn from your mistakes.

A positive attitude also greatly aids in problem solving. It is a great asset in being open-minded to formulating ideas, solutions, and strategies. People like to be associated with those who are positive. Misery loves company, and positive people want to be with encouraging individuals, not the negative ones. Now remember that you will have good and bad days, and sometimes you won't be able to distinguish which is which.

With a positive attitude, every day is a good one. Have you ever known a successful leader with a negative attitude? Adopting this principle is a key to becoming an effective leader. Remember your team will generally adopt and mirror your attitude and actions. However, I have another point of caution. People can easily detect false enthusiasm. Practicing passion can be internal as well as external. Only you can determine what is best for you. You are encouraged to attempt both. Don't overdo it. Begin with mentally practicing enthusiasm. Try it for an hour at a time. Later attempt it for a half-day, a full day, and so on. It is a good habit to develop.

During the self-improvement course, we were assigned reading requirements. The required three books dealt with overcoming worry, winning friends, and influencing people as well as learning the art of effective communications. If I only learned one key concept from the books, that is one more than I had when I began. I decided to apply what I had learned. Again my self-confidence grew a little more.

My biggest challenge at this point in my personal development was breaking my worry habit. It was extremely difficult to end the workday with a drive home lasting a few minutes and completely disengage my business concerns when I walked into my residence. This was more of a mental challenge than I had ever encountered. I don't believe you can fully separate your thoughts, especially when, on the road to career fulfillment, you need time to mentally assess your day and evaluate what you could have done better.

I found that one of the most effective means of reducing worry is to insist that your family has its evening meal together. When you ask your wife and children about their day, you disengage from your work matters. Listen to what they have to say. Show a sincere interest in them. Ask them questions. Dinner table discussion can redirect your thoughts and build a strong family. Your family feels that you care about them and what is happening in their lives. Your children get better grades, and your wife feels supported. You are opening lines of communication, which is important in a well-functioning family. Your goal should be to try to carry your discussion beyond the table. Taking an interest in them becomes their motivation to do well.

At this point in my career path, I embraced the concept that you can control some things and other things that you cannot. For example, you cannot control the weather, but you can regulate how you prepare for it. You cannot control regulations, but you can manage how you comply.

I applied a step-by-step mental process to curb my worries. Could I control certain events? I can influence how I deal with them. Worry can lead to a negative disposition, while enthusiasm is the predecessor to being positive. I used an easy solution to my concerns by first asking myself what was the worst result that could happen. Once I accepted the worst, then I built upon that. Over time, my worry habit lessened.

My wife has said many times that she envies how I can fall asleep so quickly and then soundly doze all night. Some believe that is a sign of a clear conscience. However, a bedtime prayer is a great aid in clearing your conscience. Prayer is also the ultimate cure to your worries. I won't say that I never had sleepless nights. However, there were few and far between.

Another reading requirement in my self-improvement course pertained to effective communications. The focus was not on public speaking but on your conversations with others. At this point, I adopted a philosophy of trying to put myself in the place of the customer when explaining a product, service, analysis, policy, concept, or procedure. I started with the basics and assumed nothing.

On rare occasions, the customer thought I was talking down to him or her. I apologized and explained that I wanted him or her to understand the basics when he or she made a fully informed decision. I frequently repeated myself with the goal of making sure the customer understood his or her choices. I wanted the customer's trust more than I wanted the sale. With trust comes strong relationships, resulting in great sales. Realizing all possible choices helps one make informed decisions. This form of service will result in great sales.

When speaking in public, the guide I used to be effective with my message is simply to know your audience and to know your subject. Allow for and anticipate questions. Always express appreciation for the opportunity. Use humor when appropriate, but stay away from jokes. Use storytelling to make your point. It's simpler than most believe. Effective storytelling is truthful but can be fictional if used as an example. Telling a story, especially if it were a real-life experience, is much easier to remember than a joke. Before you speak, take a deep breath, and conscientiously think about speaking slowly. Being an effective speaker is not as difficult as people have been led to believe if you follow these simple recommendations.

Getting back to the basics, when the company president and some other investors bought a company in another community, I was requested to fill in a few days a week until a permanent manager was found. The company was located in a very small town. Once again, I found myself outside my comfort zone. I found the community to be very welcoming, almost like a large family.

Over time, some of the community members contacted my company president and requested I be named the manager. Thus the offer was made to me. At this time, I had a family to think about, along with the risk of moving. I also hesitated because of the community size but accepted the challenge mainly because of my loyalty to the owners and the opportunity to be somewhat independent. My wife was accustomed to frequent moves, having grown up in the environment of a career navy father. She was excited and supportive of the move. After all, it was a career advancement.

It turned out to be a very good decision. Everyone in the community cared for and supported each other. I also had a college friend in the school district who helped me network and make new friends. The first summer that our family lived there, the community celebrated their centennial. This provided us with opportunities for new friendships and more networking opportunities. To this day, I have maintained strong friendships with many in that unique community.

As the new branch manager, I discovered a new challenge. The company had a conservative reputation. Therefore, public relations weren't the best, especially when the community did not know the new owners, all living outside the community.

One of the best ways to improve your reputation is to get involved in the community. After all, I was in the relationship business. Relationships result in company sales and growth. I joined the Lions Club and became president. The Lions Club constructed a new meeting building. I participated in the men's golf league. I ran the chains and down markers for the high school football games. I played in a men's basketball league. I ran the scoreboard for the home high school boys' basketball games. I attended the local fish fry, played cards with the guys, and did couples' bowling.

I placed myself in a position of accessibility and made many friends. Using my sales background, I know that relationships result in company loyalty and growth. Over time, the company's reputation improved, I believe, mainly because of visibility, accessibility, and community involvement. The company was giving back to the surrounding area. The staff knew all the customers by name and made them feel very welcomed.

I want to emphasize the importance of community involvement. It takes effort and sacrifice. Do not join any organization unless you commit to be active. Many join an organization as a résumé builder. And don't fool yourself. Your fellow members can see right through you. If you are active, then you will develop more leadership skills. Don't be afraid to step outside your comfort zone, one stride at a time. The value of your business dealings is fundamentally based upon relationships. Even if you make a mistake, the customer is inclined to forgive because he or she knows you and likes doing business with you.

Another lesson was learned from this experience. The company had no major problems. However, two staff members never got along. They were good with customers, knew their job responsibilities, and performed them well, but they despised each other, mostly, I believe, from envy. Sometimes their spats evolved into a distraction. Both expected me to intervene and become a referee. I believed that once you intervene, then it will always be expected. The ultimate goal is for a final resolution. I was uneasy that their spats might overflow and negatively affect the company culture.

When I finally realized that something must be done, I called them together for a conference. I expressed my disappointment with both of them and asked for a remedy. When they produced none, then I had no choice but to issue an ultimatum. Either they work it out, or I will need to make a replacement. It would be for two people and not one. Both would be gone because they were contaminating company culture.

From that point on, I don't believe they ever worked things out, but I like to think they were much better at concealing their dislike for each other. I learned it is better to ask for a remedy before issuing an ultimatum. They had the chance for input.

About five years into that management position, I received a phone call with a new opportunity to move to a slightly larger community and manage a somewhat bigger company. After careful consideration, my wife and I decided to take another risk and relocate the family again. This new community had a little different personality as we were experiencing a systemic economic crisis. Unknown to me at the time of the job offer acceptance, the external crisis situation would result in significant losses and cause the company to approach insolvency.

It appeared that the risk my family took might be catastrophic. We second-guessed our choice. The new challenge was not so much public relations like the previous operation, but the potential insolvency issue. Again we made new friends but were somewhat mistrusted and despised because of the economic crisis. I needed to start over. The company had to terminate its relationship with many of the customers or be prepared for even greater losses.

What the company had in its favor was truly great company ownership by a family who was sensitive to public opinion, caring, and favorably looked upon by the community. We had to improve our potential insolvency issue by getting most of our customers to make good on their commitments. To engage their cooperation, which in some cases involved partial or entire liquidation, was a challenge. I had to persuade some customers to do what was needed—that is, liquidate unnecessary assets in order to reduce debt and thus decrease interest-borrowing costs. I aspired for a win-win result. I again became committed to community involvement. My goal was to get to know the populace and for them to get to know me by being accessible. The staff was great but had a job to do in a difficult systemic economic crisis. The situation caused more out-of-comfort-zone anxieties.

As previously mentioned, when discussing alternatives with the customer, I learned that everyone has a different motivation point.

Some needed to be consoled, while others required a scolding or challenge. Again, the goal was to persuade our customers to do what we would like them to do but get them to feel it was their idea. Both the customer and the company could win with this approach. We may be able to avoid insolvency, and they could stay in business by pursuing a compromise.

I had to be patient, truthful, and open about their situation. I hated what had to be done but learned great lessons from the experience. Again, at the end of every day, I asked myself what I could have done better. I regret that my family sometimes experienced ridicule and were the subject of some poor jokes. I also regret the stress experienced by the customers, the great staff and their families, and the awesome owners. All of this was worth it because there were positive outcomes for the customers, and in time, the families were proud of how they grew from adversity. My leadership skills also grew.

At the same time that I was dealing with an economic crisis, I learned another guiding principle regarding first impressions. The philosophy is that you don't get a second chance for a first impression. Always remember that a firm handshake and eye contact says a lot about your self-confidence. A positive first impression can be something as simple as being well groomed to arriving early for a meeting. I learned years ago to operate on what is called "Lombardi time."

Vince Lombardi, the famed Green Bay Packer coach, had his team adopt what he called Lombardi time, which meant that when a meeting time was announced, one was always expected to arrive fifteen minutes early. His theory was that if one would adopt this philosophy, it greatly adds to one's organizational skills and speaks volumes about one's enthusiasm and, ultimately, leadership potential. It also gives one some leeway in the event he or she encounters an unexpected happening, like a flat tire or a traffic accident. In small towns, especially in times of stress, many will watch your every move in hopes of discovering a weakness or flaw in your character. First impressions, early arrivals, a firm handshake, eye contact, a smile, and a hello are all influential in your first steps to credibility.

To emphasize this further, I am reminded of an experience that I had at a barbershop many years prior. When in college I was invited to be a guest for the weekend with a new friend. After arriving at his home and being introduced to his mother, he invited me to meet his dad at his place of business. His dad was a barber. At the barbershop, his dad asked me if I knew what two things influences one's subconscious first impression of another. After conceding that I had no idea, he revealed that it was one's hair and shoes. He explained that your hair doesn't necessarily need to be freshly cut. It just needed to be well groomed. Your shoes should be clean and polished . I rationalized that his answer was because he was a barber and this would naturally promote this his hair-cutting business. I always remembered this, and at this job, I experienced its long lasting effect on me.

I had a salesperson in my office one day presenting the virtues of his product. He looked professional with vested suit and nice tie. He was clean-shaven and well groomed. He had my attention. I was very impressed until he sat back in the chair and crossed his legs. And then I noticed his shoes. They were scuffed and dirty. I mean, really scuffed up and dirty. My favorable first impression was gone, along with his credibility. My impression of him was likened to a balloon losing its air.

I remembered that experience and frequently share it with others, especially today's youth. At that exact moment, I became a believer in the subconscious "hair and shoes" first impression. The salesperson did not get the sale. He still may not have been successful with clean shoes, but he would have been closer to his goal. Someone recently told me that the "hair and shoes" philosophy mirrors a principle of discipline that the military uses.

After about five years, I was again contacted regarding yet another great opportunity in running a much larger operation in a county seat community. The town was slightly bigger in population than my hometown, and a great number of shareholders, none of which owned more than 10 percent of the company, owned the operation. It seemed like a risk that my family should take. After all, with so many local owners referring customers and a growing, highly profitable organization, how could one fail?

The decision became difficult because my current owners were great to work for. We were making friends and starting to build a good company culture. I accepted the position after participating in the interview process. This was another risk and outside of my comfort zone. My wife and children were instrumental in pursuing the opportunity. Our son was graduating from high school, and our daughter was beginning junior high. The timing was right.

Once I joined the organization, I encountered a whole new set of challenges. The company had no public relations issues and no problems with their customers. The company was experiencing great growth and profits. My first step in gaining acceptance was to utilize the lessons learned as a foundation from which to build a favorable culture and grow the business. I tried to create a favorable first impression, practiced enthusiasm, became acquainted with the staff, joined civic organizations, and listened. I did a lot of listening.

My first challenge was to attempt to develop a strong relationship with the second-in-command, whom I sensed, although denied, deep down really wanted my position. I learned that you can reach out to someone, but if he or she won't reciprocate, then there is not much you can do except be patient. I understood the disappointment. I chose to listen, offer support, and, to the best of my ability, trust the other key members of the management team, most of which were under an employment contract and were not defined under our state laws as employees at will. There are only a few circumstances by which you can make a staff change, and change for the sake of change is not one of them when a staff member is under an employment contract. It is very unusual in this industry for upper management and anyone who is not the CEO/president to be under contract.

Two others were also under contract. To terminate a staff member who had an employment contract and make personnel changes would invite litigation and cause the organization irreparable harm financially and to your reputation. This is important because it can delay the implementation of the new philosophies, especially when there is a staff resistance to change. I opted to be patient and work on my adaptability to them rather than them acclimating to me. Once I gained their trust, then I could begin to mold them and gently influence change.

My second challenge was dealing with an internal conflict. The management team was divided and feuding. I did not take sides. I soon discovered that either side thought I was against them when I gave them no indication of favoritism. They went to the board to request a vote of no confidence. The board declined and affirmed the continuing support of the CEO. The team then apologized. I forgave and continued focusing on the future. Their actions were not sufficient legal cause for a change in personnel. Again, I did receive some apologies, which I accepted, forgave, and moved on.

One of my directors shared with me that before I was hired, there were many a moment when personnel issues would come before the board. After my hiring and initiation of a process to improve the culture, no personnel issues were requested for board review except the aforementioned situation and two terminations in a span of twenty-five years.

Another challenge was the inherited expectation of the continued expectation of the predecessor's management style. The staff previously had two bosses. If they didn't get what they wanted from one, then they went to the other. Finally one of the bosses resigned, which afforded me this opportunity. The boss that left was very hands-on. I was told that his management style was one of being involved in almost every decision. There is nothing incorrect with this approach. In fact, it was traditional. However, mine was different. The staff was unaccustomed to be allowed the autonomy to make decisions on their own.

Once again, a new set of challenges faced me. How do you motivate a staff, which are set in their ways, to embrace a new management style? I needed to guide them in the art of decision making. By the way, the second boss retired shortly after my hiring and was replaced, but not in a leadership position.

I began my journey with the new company by reviewing my lessons learned and working to improve the organization and myself. I was confident that over time I would have the opportunity to change personnel. I needed to be patient. Again, the willingness to endure played a key. I learned that once you look for the good in others, you will find the best in yourself. Try it. It works. It is also a key component in developing a positive attitude.

Again I employed my values of being early to work, doing the worst jobs, and working longer hours than others did. My enthusiasm, both internally and externally, and sustaining a positive attitude was my main focus. I tried to control negative thinking, including criticism and complaining. Remember that the best method of control is first self-realization when you are in a negative mode. When negativism creeps and raids my attitude, it was changed immediately. Do not allow negativity to grow and control you. It will eat you up like a cancer.

Another key principle is that organization creates a favorable impression. I also continued my focus on breaking the worry habit. I listened. At this early time in my employment, I was blessed with an awesome secretary/administrative assistant who kept me organized, on task, and in control of my worrying. My family was very supportive, especially when working evenings and weekends.

I always wore a tie and white shirt with a suit. I polished my shoes frequently and even kept a shoeshine brush in my desk. I attempted to look professional with an emphasis on my physical appearance and attire. I was once told that you should dress for the job you want and not the job you have.

I occupied the office in the front of the building so I could enjoy eye contact and a wave at our customers when the opportunity presented itself. I found many customers stopping in my office just to visit. I reminded myself continually that I was in a relationship business and that our customers had other choices. Our goal was to make their experience with our company so enjoyable that they would not hesitate in recommending us to another. We called them our "raving fans."

I joined a civic organization and ultimately accepted a number of invitations to work on various boards. I played in a golf league and basketball at the YMCA, and I accepted various responsibilities at our church. I became active in our economic development organization. The community involvement resulted in new acquaintances and continued networking.

Early in my tenure and after I felt comfortable that I knew the staff and they had accepted me, an outside consultant persuaded the company to perform a market survey, which also included a culture review. The results of the market survey indicated that our organization was the business of choice with high customer service satisfaction. That was the good news. The flip side was that on a scale of 1 to 5, with 5 being the best, the staff satisfaction working for the company only had a composite rating of 2.8. There was a lot of room for improvement. In order to sustain a high customer satisfaction rating, the company culture needed to improve. And so my journey in some ways begins and continues in other ways.

The new challenge was how to improve a culture in an environment that was infected by an internal conflict while dealing with key members of the staff who were under contract and dearly beloved and worshiped by their customer base? What about considerations for maintaining high growth, profitability, and market share? How do you unify? What sacrifices are you and the staff willing to make for the long-term benefit of the company?

What was needed was the creation of a common purpose or goal or any agreeable commonality. It is very important that your staff develop pride in your organization. The general public doesn't care about your profitability, growth, market share, and dividend rate. However, when your company supports the community, the public will sit up and notice and then compliment your staff. It doesn't hurt when the public passes along their favorable impression of management, leadership, and the company giving back to the community. Credibility, as small as it was, began to be established. Staff pride and cooperation began to blossom. Your staff doesn't care what you know until they know that you care.

You need to understand that a part of the credibility process is the emphasis on commitments and integrity. Once you say you are going to do something, you better do it because others are always looking for flaws in your character. I am big on working hard and smart, doing the worst jobs, and being the first at work and the last to go home. I needed to work on finding just one little thing that the staff could agree upon and begin the unity process.

So where do we begin? What do we do? It was going to be almost impossible to change the attitudes of many who were long term and very set in their ways. To a great degree, the individual members of the management team were cognizant of their contribution to the success of the company. What they didn't understand was that long-term success would require more cooperation and team unity. As it is said, "You can lead a horse to water, but you can't make it drink." I needed to set a good example. In other words, "Say what you'll do, and do what you say." I needed to be the best I could be. I decided it may be more effective for me to somewhat adapt to them and their ways than expecting everyone to change. Here is what I did, and I suggest you do the same.

You need to perform a self-assessment. And your first assignment in self-assessment is simple and takes place outside the company. Try this exercise. Walk through a shopping mall, on a busy sidewalk, through a public terminal, or anywhere there are many people. Observe the faces, especially the face of a person who is by himself or herself. Look at this person's lips. Is the position neutral, smiling, or frowning? Most are neutral or slightly frowning. Does the face of those you observe influence your impression of this individual?

So what do you feel when you see someone not on a phone or engaged in conservation who has a smile on his or her face? Yes, just walking alone with no phone or reading material, but just a simple smile on his or her face. This is a rarity. Wouldn't you like to get to know this person? Do you wonder if this individual talks with a smile on his or her face too? Wouldn't you like to determine why he or she is so positive? Why does this person seem to be carefree? Now consider those who are carrying a frown. Which would you like to get to know?

Like a magnet, I am attracted to those wearing a smile. I really wonder what makes them tick. Why are they smiling? Is it because they are always positive, and if so, what makes them that way? They are content. Are you content with your life?

There is a story about two dogs that walked out of a small house at the same time. With its tongue hanging out, one was as happy as a lark with a big smile on its face. The second dog came out looking troubled and grumpy. The person who saw both decided to venture into the house to see what happened and why the difference. To the person's surprise, one hundred mirrors filled the house. The happy dog saw a hundred happy, smiling dogs. The other dog saw a hundred reflections of troubled and grumpy dogs. What do you see? Practice smiling, and soon facial muscle memory will ultimately influence your attitude. Your team will reflect back your mind-set. It takes seventeen muscles to smile and forty-two muscles to frown.

I am also curious what makes others frown. I see it as a challenge to turn that frown upside down. My wife and I love to take a grumpy restaurant server, for example, and get this person to smile and laugh and enjoy his or her experience with us. We always enjoy the challenge of reversing one's attitude. The server ultimately feels good about himself or herself, and we feel we might have contributed to a part of his or her day that was positive. Most customers would merely accept that a grumpy, unhappy person served them and that the service was poor. We love the challenge. Now if a happy, positive server serves us, it makes us want to return. A positive attitude plays a major role in great service.

Your goal with your staff should be the same, to motivate them to move their frown to a neutral position and then to encourage those with a neutral position to a smile. Does your staff smile when they look at you? Why or why not? Are they a reflection of you? Remember—your face, especially your mouth and lips, carries your attitude. Your face plays a significant role in your body language. Your body language broadcasts messages.

Now take the reflection test. Go to a mirror and look at yourself. What does your mouth and lips reflect about you? Try smiling and carrying that grin for one minute as you walk through your house or workplace. If you can do one minute, then try a second. Others will surely be curious as to why you are smiling. You will discover that they have a desire to want get to know you based upon your smile. Do you project positivity? Your positivity will attract people, while your negativity will only attract those who you do not necessarily want to be associated with.

"Smile in the mirror. Do that every morning and you'll start to see a big difference in your life," once said Yoko Ono.

Once you attract others, then the next question is, do people find you easy to talk with? You carry on a good conversation with someone by mostly listening. Ask yourself, do people really want to be around me? When they do, you have taken a major step in leadership. Be accessible and watch your company culture grow and your turnover decline.

As previously noted, an approach to positivity is, of course, to avoid those who are negative, the complainers, and those with cynical attitudes. Seek those who are enthusiastic and positive and do not complain. I somewhat appreciate complainers, but only if they can offer a solution to that which they are complaining. You then can begin cultivating a positive attitude.

It is important to cultivate a positive attitude by beginning with practicing enthusiasm. Don't overdo it. Enthusiasm cultivates an open attitude and a willingness to be open to new ideas. Overenthusiasm is like having a new puppy. They lick your face and are excited and happy to be with you. However, you can only take so much face licking before you push away the puppy. Avoid the "new puppy" syndrome.

Second, be aware of your thoughts and attitudes. Avoid negative thinking, being critical, and complaining. If you can become self-aware of your attitude, you have taken one very important step in cultivating a positive mental attitude. Try to go one hour without being negative in thoughts or oral expression. Just one hour. If you can do one hour, then try two. When you complete two, then try a half-day. Next, why not a full day? When a full day, then try two, a week, a half-month, a month, and so on. Avoid criticism and complaining both in thoughts, action, and conversation.

Your attitude will become contagious, resulting in admiration by others and more enjoyment of your life, your family, and your job. More importantly, your positive attitude allows you to rebound from life's disappointments and challenges. How you handle adversity influences your admiration by others and your leadership.

Another recommended principle is that of being a responder, not a reactor. Think before you speak. Work smart. Be positive. Be a leader. Visualize the type of person and ultimately the leader you want to be. Embrace previous recommendations, and you will ultimately inspire others. A special note: be patient. Your transformation may take years. Embrace just one guiding principle, and then when you feel it is somewhat perfected, move to another. Over time, you will become the leader you envisioned.

The third point in cultivating a positive attitude is to never expect recognition for your personal achievements. Always presume ingratitude. Having expectations of recognition will serve only as a disappointment when you don't receive it and can lead to an obstacle in your growth in positivity. I emphasize that anytime your expectations are exceeded and you are in some way recognized for your achievement, then you will genuinely be surprised and appreciate your moment in the spotlight more than ever. Always expect ingratitude.

When you are recognized for an achievement, it is important to respond strategically by strongly giving others all the credit. Do it sincerely. With that approach, others will work harder, and you will achieve even greater results and more recognition. Deep down, others know who really deserves all the credit. You are now becoming a true leader.

The next point of emphasis is about forgiveness. Don't let a grudge become baggage and an obstacle toward your positivity and leadership goals. The sooner you forgive, the quicker you can get on the road to culture success. I know there are those who are not too fond of me. Nevertheless, I endeavor to be friendly toward these people. One of two things will happen, both of which are positive.

Either they will forgive you and become your friend, or they will despise you even more, allowing negativity to lead to their self-destruction. This will become their burden and serve as an obstacle to their positivity path. They become their own roadblock on their path to promotion. You, on the other hand, have taken the higher path toward leadership.

Another guiding principle deals with commitments. Too many times, I see people renege on one commitment because something they perceive to be better comes along. Remember to say yes only if you really want to. What would you do if your close friend invited you to dinner to celebrate a special occasion and, after accepting, your supervisor invited you to be his guest at a big community social event at an exclusive country club? How would you handle that situation? A characteristic of a strong leader is one who lives up to his or her commitments—that is, "Say what you do, and do what you say." This is another guiding characteristic of a leader.

It is vital to understand the difference between character and integrity. Character is how you act when everyone is watching; integrity is how you act when no one is watching. Here is a good example of integrity: you drive into a parking ramp, stop at the gate, and take a ticket. You return a few hours later to discover that the exit gate is wide open. You ask yourself if the gate is stuck open or meant to be for free parking. What would most people do? One with high integrity would still go to the redemption machine and pay for a validation ticket. Others, thinking no one was watching, would drive out without paying, rationalizing it was probably meant for free parking. What would others do if they had knowledge they were on camera?

Remember—in the world we live in, cameras are everywhere. You entered the ramp intending to pay. Without signage or notice of free parking, then you should plan to pay. That is what I call a guiding principle. Act as though you are being recorded. Act as though you are on a camera. You will soon discover the difference between integrity and character.

In conclusion, your ultimate guiding principle should be to live your life in such a fashion that if someone ever said anything bad about you, then everyone would believe that it is just not true.

In summary, some of the following principles are recommended:

1. Conduct a self-evaluation.
2. Develop a strong work ethic.
3. Set a good example; be organized.
4. Observe success examples.
5. Embrace a service culture.
6. Smile.
7. Don't be afraid of backward steps.
8. Ask yourself what you learned today and whether you could have done or said it better.
9. Show appreciation for your family.
10. Take a self-improvement course; read a self-improvement book.
11. Remember what true happiness is.
12. Avoid negative people.
13. Practice enthusiasm.
14. Remember that you don't get a second chance for a first impression.
15. Always use a firm handshake.
16. Use good eye contact.
17. Operate on Lombardi time.
18. Learn from your mistakes.
19. Remember your hair and shoes.
20. Kick the worry habit.
21. Learn effective communications skills.
22. Develop a positive attitude.
23. Ask for solutions or choices before revealing your recommendation.
24. Dress for the job you want, not the job you have.
25. Say what you'll do, and do what you say.
26. Expect ingratitude.
27. Learn to forgive.

28. Honor your commitments.
29. Know the difference between character and integrity; act like you're being filmed.
30. Live your life in such a fashion that if someone says something bad about you, then everyone would believe that it is just not true.

As you can observe, the recommendations are lengthy, and each would probably warrant a publication by itself. Nevertheless, embrace them one at a time. Start with the easiest concept to adopt. And once understood, then move to another. Be patient. Stay determined. Take one step at a time.

The next step in building a strong culture is getting to know each member of the staff better. Their trust, confidence, and support are essential. I needed to earn it and not to expect it to be automatically given. I decided to adapt to them first before expecting them to acclimate to me.

Positive, happy people attract positive, happy people. Negative people attract negative people and repel positive people.

If you really want to embrace these recommendations to better yourself, then you will find a way. If not, then you'll find an excuse. If you really want to be a good leader and enhance your company culture, then you will find a way. If not, then you'll find an excuse. Remember to start your journey by doing what is the easiest for you to embrace and continually build your skill set from there.

CHAPTER 2

You and the Staff Individually …
Assembly Required

Now that you are working on being the best you can be, it is time to focus on your individual relationships with your staff. You are reminded that in order to enhance your culture, three parts need emphasis. You and your individual staff relationships are the second part.

To build on your individual staff relationships, you must gain their respective individual confidence. You should get to know the staff and their families. All business is based upon relationships, whether it is with your customers or your staff. So how well do you know your staff? Do you know their likes and dislikes, their hobbies, their significant others and where they work, the names and ages of their children, and so on?

I learned from experience that people really like to talk about their families, especially their children and grandchildren. You are encouraged to attend their children's extracurricular activities. Show a sincere interest in them. Congratulate them on their performance and effort. Observe the family pride of participation. You will be amazed how accepted you become and how your professional relationships develop.

When you are getting to know the individual likes and dislikes of your staff, it is a good time to better understand their values. You will be surprised how much members of your staff are willing to open up.

The goal is to open lines of communication. You want to be trusted; you want to trust them. Trust will lead to an open door policy, which is good for morale. Try it. It works.

Over time, you will get acquainted with their friends. Who they select as friends will say a lot about their values. People are judged by the company they keep. The same goes for you. My wife and I have been blessed to select real down-to-earth friends with great reputations and awesome values.

When being introduced to a staff member's family or friends, and whether or not in the presence of that particular person, accentuate the attributes and values of that individual. You can always find something positive to say about anyone. Brag him or her up. You will be surprised how compliments in this person's presence become an even greater incentive for that particular staff member to perform at an even higher level. This concept also works with your children. Say something positive about your child to a relative or friend. Make sure the child is within earshot. It keeps him or her motivated.

A few years prior to my retirement, I volunteered to teach a business course in middle school. I got to know many of the students and their teacher very well. At the year-end awards assembly, I was invited to announce the finalist for the eighth-grade citizenship awards. Ten finalists (five boys and five girls) were recognized. I had the privilege of then announcing the boy and girl winner. My message to the full auditorium was simple: "Live your life in such a fashion that if anyone ever says anything bad about you, then everyone will think it is untrue."

A few days later, we invited those ten finalists and their adviser, Rachel M., to come to our company boardroom for a special-recognition catered lunch. Our company announced that a public library book would be dedicated in the name of the boy and girl citizenship winners respectively, as donated by our company.

In promoting discussion, I asked the ten finalists a question. "What was it about your selection that distinguished you from all the other students?"

Two answers were prominent. They said they had good parenting and selected good friends. Their selection of good friends was an important factor in their minds. Their friends had strong moral values. You are who you associate with.

The same principle applies to your staff. You need to heighten your awareness of who your staff associates with. It says a great deal about them. Again you and they are a reflection of the company that is kept.

I made time during the day to occasionally visit with the staff individually, preferably in their offices and not mine. Staff members always feel more comfortable when they are in the comfort of their workstations or offices. I wanted to know how they were doing and what they needed to make their jobs more rewarding, as well as less complicated.

During my first months on the job, I requested a one-on-one with each staff member. I invited them to my office. After that, I was reluctant to call anyone to my office, as everyone had a tendency to assume the worst, especially if I closed my office door. My goal was to be very accessible. I always tried to keep my office door open, even in discussion. Going to the staff one-on-one at their workspaces eliminated a wrongful supposition and actually is a significant step in building individual staff relationships.

I want to emphasize one detail. When you are visiting an associate staff member, always talk to this person at his or her eye level. Sit down; don't stand. You need to make this person feel as though he or she is an equal. You will be surprised how much this person will open up to you. It may take some time, but remember that patience plays a vital role in growing and enhancing your company culture.

You need to understand the responsibilities of each. How do they do what they do, and what are their challenges? Do you know what they are? Who are the leaders among your staff? Who are the producers? Who do you trust? Who do you like to be around? Why? Who do you go to when you need help? Do all your staff members have the same values? Are they cognizant of their strengths and weaknesses? What are their likes and dislikes? What were your first impressions of them as they evaluated you? Is everybody on your team heading in the same direction?

Now, over time I accepted that not everyone would embrace my management style and me. There were probably even those who just did not care for me. However, that doesn't mean that I can't like them. I learned years before that unjust criticism just might be a compliment in disguise. So I always tried to look for the good in others. One of my guiding philosophies is that when you look for the good in others, then you will find the best in yourself. I also believe it is important to forgive and not let dispute and dislike become a burden or baggage that weighs on your attitude. It will slowly eat at you like a cancer. You need to move forward and attempt to learn the rationale for their attitude toward you. Once you understand their reasoning, then you can better deal with improving your relationship.

I try to practice the golden rule, or "Do unto others as you would have them do unto you." I trusted everyone until I was given a reason not to. I never rushed to judgment of an associate's behavior and did my best to understand this person's core beliefs and values and what made him or her tick.

It is difficult to move forward and develop your staff if they were poor hires to begin with. One important point of emphasis is dealing with hiring. Most interviews focused on the job and the applicant's job background. I tried to take note of the applicant's interpersonal skills and, as much as could be determined, his or her values. I particularly focused on my first impression, the person's positive attitude, and his or her sense of humor. I can teach the business, but it is extremely difficult to impart positive interpersonal skills. It can be done, but it is much easier to self-improve than improve another.

Their values, although difficult to judge in a job interview, were a very key element. I believe there will be situations in the workplace that require quick decisions. Surveys indicate that the staff member may panic and forget proper procedure. In a panic circumstance or crisis, a staff member is likely to rely upon his or her moral values to influence the decision. In theory, a staff member will likely make a correct decision when reverting to his or her moral values in time of crisis. If this person has good moral values, then the odds are great that he or she will take the right action. So how do you know if this person has good moral values? Again, get to know this individual, along with his or her family, friends, likes, and dislikes.

Never forget the basics. Don't underestimate the impact of saying "please" and "thank you" and the use of a firm handshake with good eye contact. Always open the door for others. Dress for the job you want, not the job you have. Always expect ingratitude. If you are confident, yet not boastful, then unjust criticism will not affect you. Always knock before you enter. And continually smile!

By getting to know your staff better, you will soon discover that you become more accepted and respected. One of the keys to getting people to like you is that you need to understand that individuals really like to talk about themselves. When you give them that opportunity, they remember the experience and feel good about you. Always do your best to not talk about yourself unless it is an experience that proves a point. People don't care what you know until they know that you care. Try using this principle, no matter if you playing golf with three strangers, you're sitting at a table with strangers at a wedding reception, and the list goes on. Get people talking about themselves.

I cannot emphasize enough the principle of asking people about their family. People are always proud of their children and grandchildren. Practice the technique of getting others to talk about themselves by simply asking your children what happened in school or your spouse about his or her day. If you teach your children the importance of getting others to talk about themselves, their fear of attending social functions greatly lessens. Most self-talkers are usually arrogant, which can be counterproductive to cultivating a positive relationship. When you can be humble, be so. If someone asks you about yourself, answer and reflect the question back to this person by asking him or her about himself or herself. You have two eyes, two ears, and only one mouth for a reason. People will have a favorable impression of you if you focus on them and not you. People may forget what you said, and persons may forget what you did, but they will never forget how you made them feel.

To begin the process of getting to know my staff, I started with the accounting/bookkeeping department because I began my career there. I talked with the manager and learned about his history and progression within the organization. To this day, twenty-six years later, I know the name of his spouse and where she worked. I sat next to a bookkeeper and shared my experience performing his same task. I met his spouse and again learned about the company history. I then spent time working with the staff at a satellite office. I discovered that one of the ladies drove a straight truck on the weekend to a livestock auction to buy hogs. I arranged to ride with her and then help load and unload the livestock. I met her husband and her daughter. I even visited her mother-in-law. So far, all the families I met were awesome.

I then made an effort to get to know the head of our frontline department. I met his spouse and children. I worked with the others on the front line and learned about them. I then went to the company officers to gain knowledge about them. I met their spouses and children. More importantly, I gave special attention when a young family member stopped by the company to visit a parent in his or her office or workplace. I took time to say hello and engage this person in conversation. My intent was to get to know the families and send the message that they were encouraged to stop in anytime. I learned their names. I even included one of their children in a company ad with me.

Another very important point is that your staff needs to believe that their family should be a higher priority. Early in my tenure, I adopted a policy of allowing staff to leave the company early in order to support a child or grandchild who was participating in an extracurricular activity. In my early management years, we even paid the staff for the time they were gone from the company. My emphasis was that their job with our company should not be their first priority. Your family and your faith would hopefully carry far more importance in your life than your job did. This philosophy helps to enhance the culture.

One of my company experiences gave me the opportunity to observe the value of staff relationships. It happened when members of our board and management team made a trip to another town to discuss the potential purchase of a vacant building. The building owner was the founder of a large and very well-known midwestern business chain.

When we landed at the airport, the owner met us and drove us to the executive offices for discussion and negotiations in his boardroom. As we were escorted through the corporate office and among the cubicles of computer workers, I couldn't help but notice the numerous times the owner stopped and asked his staff about their families. The owner was retired but had access to a meeting room. I observed that his interest was sincere and he recited all the staff family members by name. I was intrigued and amazed. I said to myself that I wanted to be able to have the same type of relationship; thus I began my effort to do so. I wanted more than ever to know my staff and their families.

I learned many years ago that your name is very important to you. Remember that repetition is the mother of memory, so you should make a conscientious effort to learn names by repeating someone's name as much as you can, especially when in conversation with that particular individual. When you use someone's name, he or she takes notice and feels important. When you are first introduced to someone, use his or her name frequently in the introduction. I have heard it said that your name is the sweetest music to your ears. People like to hear their name spoken. Don't be afraid to admit if you forgot one's name. It says you're human.

My next goal was to determine how to incorporate developing the staff while improving my management style and myself. I like self-improvement books, so I came across what I consider a must read, *The One-Minute Manager* by Ken Blanchard. At this point in time, the corporate buzz word was "empowerment." I began utilizing the principles I learned from the book as a guide to focus on the doctrine of empowerment. I reminded myself that the staff had grown accustomed to decision making by others, particularly upper management. My process was time consuming but easy for the staff to understand.

When a staff member would come to me for guidance regarding a situation, I would ask him or her to name all the possible solutions. I then would ask this person for what he or she believed to be the best solution. Most of the time, I would conclude our discussion by asking this person if his or her final recommendation were in line with our mission statement, values, and objectives. I emphasized that if the results were not what was expected, then we would learn from it, get better, and try another choice or direction. My point is that we will learn from our mistakes and empowerment means more than relinquishing authority. Empowerment also means teaching the art of decision making.

Now I will be the first to admit that not everyone learns from his or her mistakes. However, when this person makes the same mistake twice, as in athletics, you need to sit this individual on the bench for a time and discuss what he or she did and needs to have learned. Now if this person makes the same mistake a third time, then he or she might be taken out of the game. This individual still remains on the team; however, he or she might lose playing time.

You need to encourage your staff to not be afraid to learn from their mistakes. If they are not afraid to make an error, then they will take a more relaxed approach and undoubtedly perform better. As their mentor, your job is to review their choices with them, along with what they learned from both their successes and mistakes. Teach someone the art of decision making, as it is to teach ownership and empowerment. It is your job to train them to be better and improve so they have the skills to fill the position. Compliments go a long way, especially in front of others. Criticism should only be noted in private.

Some in leadership positions immediately grasped the concept, while others were mistrusting. They were suspicious that I was looking for someone to blame if things didn't work out or maybe even the opportunity for me to take most of the credit. Again, when

I made a mistake, I immediately admitted it without blaming others. I even shared my mistakes and what I learned. In time and over a long period, they started to experience a change in culture. I gave the staff the credit for all successes, and I shared in the blame for their mistakes. If you make a mistake, it means you are trying. Even if I had a personal success or a special achievement, I always found a means to give credit to others. In time, the staff came to realize that we were all working together. This helped promote unity and grow the company into a more positive culture.

You must continually take time to be with staff. Another personal objective was to send a nonverbal message that I have an open door policy. I wanted to hear their views. I wanted to be fully accessible. I did not wait for the staff to come to me. It is vital to continually make rounds and visit your staff. Sometimes a staff visit can just be a simple "good morning" and "how are you today?" When the staff member said "good morning" in return and affirmed he or she was doing good, then I would ask this person why he or she wasn't "awesome."

Over time, the response was "awesome," and this person's attitude became more positively awesome. As a powerful leader, every day should begin with a good morning to everyone you meet in the company. Take a minute and walk through your department or company just to greet everyone. This is a simple act but very impactful. However, I was very cautious in socializing with the staff one-on-one for fear that others might think I would favor that one person. My advice is to only be social with staff if it includes everyone at an all-company or all-department function.

In addition, I always made time to greet and interact with the customers. I knew the staff was observing my customer interaction. Public opinion greatly influences their pride in leadership. I applied the same "get to know" principles to the customers I used with the staff. I got the customers talking about themselves and mostly their families. My goal was to get them to feel good about our interaction and their visit to our company.

Throughout my staff relationships, I learned the power of what I call an "effective vocabulary for action," or an EVA. When I needed to have a task performed, I never asked the staff member if he or she "could" do something. I asked this person if he or she "would" do something. After all, would you ask someone if he or she could marry you, or would this person marry you? The use of the word "would" requests definitive action. The use of the word "could" invites someone to just answer regarding his or her ability but not his or her commitment to perform the task. The question seems to mean the same, but the manner in which the staff accepts your request is quite different. "Would" promotes a positive action while "could" is more of an inquiry. Try to eliminate the word "could" and substitute the word "would."

I also never told a staff member they he or she was "wrong." I eliminated the word "wrong" from my vocabulary and replaced it with the term "mistaken." If I disagreed with another, telling this person that he or she is "mistaken" keeps his or her mind open to my point of view. If I tell this individual that he or she is "wrong," then it seemed that he or she became defensive and entrenched even more in his or her position. The word "wrong" results in an obstacle to compromise.

Another powerful concept to embrace is eliminating the word "I" and replacing it with the word "we." When you're talking about what is happening in your company, don't say "I" am going to do; say "we" are going to do. "We" implies that a strategy, an effort, or whatever is going to happen will be a team effort. "We" did this. Not "I" did this. It promotes the team concept.

While working for a company is a serious undertaking, you must find methods to inject humor into your daily operations. I don't care for jokes or gags because they are too easily misinterpreted. Don't go there. I like to kid the staff. Over time, the staff returns your kidding with their own. It brings you closer. Even using nicknames when appropriate can make working together a fun experience.

Here is an example of one acquiring a nickname. A vendor gave Jim M., a vice president of the company and a key member of the management team, a golf shirt. Jim, a great golfer, has a great sense of humor. We started kidding him about the shirt, which was a pale yellow. One of the staff called the color "buttercup." So you guessed it. From that day forward, he was branded with the nickname Buttercup. It is so contrary to his personality, but he cracks up every time we use it.

Your relationship with your staff is a key to enhancing your company culture. The most commonly accepted and maybe overused point of focus is that "the customer is number one." Is that really true? Maybe you should embrace the concept that your staff is number one. With a great positive staff, they will easily take care of the customer. Both the staff and the customer will experience a sense of priority. So once you have improved your one-on-one relationship with each and every staff member, then what's next?

Start small with one of the simple concepts, and then build upon it. Next we move to chapter 3, you and the entire staff.

CHAPTER 3

You and the Entire Staff as a Group

How do we get everyone on the same page with a sense of self-investment and cooperation for maximum results? What needs to be completed to make our organization better? What was our culture all about? It seemed that strategic planning was necessary. The management team and the board of directors agreed to hire an outside marketing firm to determine our market positions and customer service rating and to assess staff satisfaction.

We then hired a consultant with expertise in this area. The consultant acquired a mailing list and sent surveys with a two-dollar award to every tenth person on the mailing list. Surveys were returned to him, who then compiled the results. It is vital to establish a baseline by which to measure any progress, including your culture. The survey response rate was close to 20 percent, which was higher than normally expected. Experts suggest that if your response rate is as high as 20 percent, then your results are statistically valid.

We discovered that our reputation was outstanding and 96 percent of those doing business would recommend us to another. Our market share was 49 percent in a small market with three other competitors. We also discovered that many respondents had more than four different relationships with our company.

As I previously discussed, the staff satisfaction survey overshadowed all those great results. The question, as previously noted, posed to them was, "On a scale of 1 to 5, with 5 being the best, how would you rate your satisfaction with working here?" The composite result was 2.8. Instead of determining the reason, which would probably result in a lot of finger-pointing, I decided to move forward and brought in a new consultant to facilitate strategic planning. Both the market and staff surveys were used as a guide.

A resource that proved to be very valuable was an employee workplace element survey, which an East Coast university conducted a few years earlier. The question was asked of the staff to rank ten workplace elements in order of importance. The question was then asked of the supervisors to rank the elements according to how they believed their staff would respond.

Some of the factors to be ranked were appreciation for work, good relationships with colleagues, good work-life balance, good relationship with supervisors, good company financial stability, opportunity for learning and career development, job security, attractive compensation package, interesting job content, communications, empathy, and company values. Supervisors ranked salary as what they believed was most important to the staff. However, by comparison, the staff said the most important element to them was communications or knowing what was happening in the company. The second most important element was that the supervisor showed empathy to the staff. Salary or the compensation package ranked eighth. This was an eye-opener. When most members of your staff leave your organization, they seem to always cite salary as the reason, which may or may not be the true explanation. So our strategic planning journey began.

We needed to determine a written strategic plan with a mission statement. Why are we here? Where are we going, and how are we going to get there? We agreed that the mission statement must be the guiding principle to strategic decision making. We identified key areas of the plan, like profitability, market share, technology, benefits, human resources, and growth. We set goals and objectives and assigned responsibilities.

It is important to note that this was a group effort and I was merely part of the group. I refused to dictate answers. I attempted to build consensus. The management team needed to feel ownership of the plan. They determined the direction. Even if I didn't fully agree with their ideas, I accepted their input and embraced their suggestions in an effort to build consensus.

When we began discussing human resources, I sat back and listened intently, hoping we could find a resolution to the disappointing 2.8 survey result. The management team decided it was important to focus on communications with an emphasis on revealing to the staff everything happening in the organization. The team felt it was important that the staff heard items from management before hearing it on the street. Open communications strategies promote trust. Trust is a key element in building a strong culture.

Two actions were the result of the plan. The first was that our organization would establish a mandatory monthly all-staff meeting and secondly, we would begin every week with a brief officer's meeting.

The mandatory meeting would have a set date and time. We chose the first Thursday of every month from seven fifteen until eight in the morning. A set agenda would be formulated that would include a very brief report from each department head. We only used the agenda as a guide to enhance the efficiency and effectiveness of the meeting. We even included the board chair, who did an excellent job providing closing remarks. Company performance would be reviewed as compared to projections. Market share would be discussed as well as information about our competitors, their products, and their performance. This was all done as a major step toward improving communications.

Using this strategy, many objectives were being obtained, including transparency and enhanced open communications. I was also proud to see the members of the management team and other presenters grow in confidence from their experience in speaking before the staff. It was rewarding to observe their growth and self-confidence as well as the overall development of all presenters, especially the management team.

It is important to note that confidentiality was emphasized at every meeting. The staff understood that a violation of confidentiality would, at a minimum, result in the future non sharing of important information. They policed themselves. If communications and sharing were important to them, then we should not have any problems, and we never did. The confidential information was never about a customer. It was usually about a company strategy, a recent audit, or our review of the strategic plan. In time, the trust between management and the staff mutually grew.

The second action item was to begin every week with a brief Monday morning officers' meeting. The agenda was simple: what was going on in the company this week, who was on vacation, what community activities we needed to be involved with, and what internal committee meetings were scheduled. At the conclusion of the meeting, officers would be e-mailed a summary with a weekly calendar of events. They in turn were to share the information with their staff. Again, the ultimate goal was to enhance communications. The weekly schedule was also posted on the company intranet.

The next goal was to promote more of a sense of staff unity and cooperation. We thought it might be best to set a common company goal and then reward the staff with a fun experience. We began with inviting the staff to a dinner at a local steak house. No spouses or board members were invited. When we completed the meal, I stood up and announced a new program with a common company goal. If the company grew to a certain level and remained there for a brief period of three consecutive business days, we would celebrate again with another complimentary meal. I didn't set a time limit because I wanted the staff to enjoy themselves so immensely that they became self-motivated to attain the next goal as quickly as possible.

The meal was meant to be fun and contain a lot of kidding. The first goal was set to be easily attainable with just normal inflation. Over time, the staff came to call this the "goal dinner." A goal dinner committee was established to set the goal. I had the power of veto, which I rarely used. I had a great deal of enjoyment debating with the committee regarding their goal-setting recommendation. Their goal always seemed too easy to attain. Nevertheless, I relented and accepted their recommendation. After all, the ultimate goal was to build staff relationships. Growing the company was important but secondary.

Over time, the dinner evolved into a fun function. New staff members were chided into making a brief speech. It became an event that everyone looked forward to attending. Once the goal was attained, the goal committee would set the time, place, and date for the meal, which was usually at a local steak house. We usually had a dinner every nine to twelve months.

In twenty-five years of goal dinners, there was never one instance of misconduct. The staff had fun but maintained their professionalism. Quite often, the next day began with smiles, a renewed appreciation for each other, and many positive comments. This was another positive step in enhancing culture.

A footnote to this is that two more competitors moved into our market, and yet our market share grew to better than 60 percent. When I retired, six companies were competing for the market. This is a great tribute to our staff and their embrace of the concept that great service would result in great sales and growth.

We also recognized the staff in unusual ways. At the mandatory monthly all-staff meeting, I discovered a great opportunity for the staff to assess progress and grow themselves. I determined the agenda so I had the authority to have the staff participate in unusual surveys. I also included a motivational quote on the agenda handout that everyone received. I am big on written agendas, which everyone had at his or her table. It was also posted on the overhead screen. The agenda contained a motivational or humorous quote of the day.

At one of the meetings, I passed a piece of paper to everyone. I asked them to complete the following:

1. Write the name of the associate who first comes to mind that is the most positive.
2. Write the name of the first associate who first comes to mind that gives the best service.

3. Write the name of the first associate who first comes to mind that is the most professional.

They were to hide their answers. They were instructed not to write their or my name. I then collected their answers, which I tabulated in private.

Now I realize that many do not like to be recognized in front of their peers, but some do. So in place of group recognition, here is what I did. When the staff showed up one month later for the next all-staff meeting, they may or may not have noticed some unusual objects on their desk or workstation. At the all staff meeting, I explained that when they arrived at work, they might notice a nice new pen on their desk/workstation, a battery, a tennis ball or many all three. If you found a pen, it meant that a colleague had nominated them at the previous meeting for being very professional. I then explained that if they found a battery, then someone had nominated them for having a very positive attitude. I explained further that the battery symbolized positivity. If you stand the battery up on its end and observed, you would notice that the positive end points upward. Such is the case for positive people. The last item was a tennis ball. If they received a tennis ball, it meant that someone nominated them for exemplary service. I reminded the staff that every tennis set begins with the serve. The server announces "service" and the competition begins. You have no game without service.

A few staff members received all three items, some one or two, and others none. I stated that the recipients had the option of proudly displaying what they received on their desk or at their workstation. Note that I did not reward the staff member with the most votes but instead recognized all nominees. I recommended at the very least they place the item(s) in their desk so, when viewed by them, they could be continually reminded of their recognition. I noticed a change in those who did not receive a token. Those who received an item had more pride and growing self-confidence. Most importantly the recognition was based upon a survey of their peers and not the CEO.

When the company was reaching a milestone in historic company growth, I promised the staff that we would do something very special. Once we attained the goal, the company paid for a weekend getaway for spouses and staff at a resort area approximately two and a half hours away. The staff and spouses or guests checked into the resort on mid-Saturday afternoon. At five o'clock, the staff was requested to meet in the lobby. We then followed a guide to a huge outdoor tent. The guide divided the group into nine teams. Spouses were included but could not be on the same team with their spouse. Each team was given a garbage can containing many unusual items. No garbage can had the same items as another. Each team was given thirty minutes to take the garbage can items and design a miniature golf hole. After each hole was completed, then a golf tournament was held. The low score was given a prize. The ultimate intent was team building and for staff members to get to know each other and their spouses better.

After garbage golf, we all retreated to dinner, a fun experience with a few speeches. The next morning, the staff was given a voucher that they could use for golf, horseback riding, shopping, and so forth. The resort gave us a late checkout. I played golf with a staff member's husband. He is a great guy, and I thoroughly enjoyed his company. Ultimately, without the realization of most of the staff, team building was elevated, and I kept my commitment to reward the staff for achievement.

Another fun, symbolic gesture to emphasize the company focus on a service culture was a lapel pin made to resemble a group of grapes, to emphasize our objective to be more of a service culture than a sales culture.

I contacted a local novelty/office supply salesperson. I requested research on finding a lapel pin of a bundle of grapes. The salesperson came back with a beautiful gold pin with purple grapes outlined in gold. It was very attractive. But why grapes? GRAPES is an acronym for "Great service Repeated with sincere Appreciation Produces Excellent Sales." The awesome lapel pins were exactly what I wanted.

When the pins arrived, I then called a meeting of only the frontline customer service staff. In private, I gave each a lapel pin and explained what the GRAPES acronym meant. Since they played a key role in implementing the service culture, I encouraged each to wear his or her pin with pride. My intent was to present other staff members with a lapel pin when I heard they had given or provided someone with great service. By the way, great service can also be achieved when a staff member or department helps another associate or work area with a matter. It was not confined to service with the customer.

When presenting a lapel pin to staff, I would not explain the symbolism or the GRAPES acronym. Instead I encouraged them to reach out to the frontline customer service staff for the meaning, who would then do so. All I would tell the recipient is that he or she was being recognized for a positive service action. The frontline customer service staff felt a sense of power that they had never experienced. It was rewarding to observe their growth as they underwent an internal importance amongst their peers not previously felt.

Now I want to emphasize that everything does not work according to intent. We all make mistakes. However, we discovered a way to put a positive twist on customer service errors. We call them SROs, or service recovery opportunities. When an error is discovered, the staff had the power to immediately correct the situation and make the customer feel good about the company. It was not unusual to have a customer state that the way we reacted would not have happened with a larger company. A negative was turned into a positive, another huge step in building a service culture. By the way, the customer became what we call a "raving fan."

Another strategy utilized in emphasizing the importance of embracing a service culture involved a book, *Raving Fans by Ken Blanchard and Sheldon Bowles*. Each member of the staff was given the book and asked to read it, which would be briefly discussed at an all-staff meeting. The staff was allowed to add their reading time to their time cards. Ultimately, when our company received a compliment, it would be shared at the all-staff meeting. We referred to the customer who gave us the compliment as a "raving fan." The staff became aware of positive customer comments and shared with each other the recognition of a raving fan. They became focused on developing raving fans.

To show the importance of family, the company annually chartered a bus to take the families and their friends to a Class A professional baseball game. The stadium provided a family picnic area, and the price of a ticket included food and refreshments. We always tried to time our trip to a game when there was a scheduled fireworks display immediately following. Again, it was a great event. Families got to know other families. It aided in intracompany relationship building, and of course, it was another step in enhancing company culture.

A final item of note relevant to staff development was in education. The company embraced the importance of education and paid for all expenses associated with conventions, conferences, and other academic programs. Spouses were encouraged to attend at company expense. The only request was that the participant would share a brief summary at the all-staff meeting of what they learned and experienced. Of course, permission to attend any conference, continuing education, or convention rested with one's supervisor.

The company also adopted a philosophy of providing complimentary tickets for each staff member and his or her spouse to attend local civic volunteer organization fund-raiser dinners. This evolved into a great marketing tool. The staff was encouraged to stay for the meal and spread out to visit with other attendees. They did not need to discuss business unless they were asked to do so. Our company is based upon service and relationships. This was a great way to enhance customer relationships and provide the staff with usually a free meal at the same time.

A fun function of the year was the company Christmas party. I did not want any staff member or my spouse to deal with the stress of planning so I handled the details. I would set the party for the first Friday of every December. We began with a social hour followed by a set menu, which later became a steak house special named after our company. Some parties included entertainment, while others incorporated fun and games. There was always a speech or two, usually by the newcomers. We always took a picture of each attendee with his or her spouse or guest as a keepsake. Board introductions were made, along with a summary of the past year's highlights. Each participant was asked to bring a gift costing no more than ten to twelve dollars. Men were to bring a man's gift; women were asked to provide a woman's gift. After the gifts were distributed, the participants were asked to display their gift and introduce themselves. The most rewarding part of the party was recognizing the individual staff for various years of service. We even had staff members who worked more than forty and fifty years for our company. This recognition promoted pride of longevity.

As a footnote to longevity, the staff turnover was very low, less than 5 percent. Lack of turnover creates efficiency. However, a little turnover does bring new ideas and enthusiasm into the company. This can be a good thing.

I have shared a few of the action items with the staff, all in the name of fun and growth through service. It is an individual journey. What worked for us may not work for you. However, focus on service was easier for the staff to embrace than the pressure of sales quotas. Attaining personal, department, and company goals rewarded the staff, who performed better because they were having fun and were more relaxed. They knew what was happening and even had a hand in determining the company direction. Service seemed to come natural. Results were greater than projections. The company culture was enhanced.

Whatever your process, do not forget the importance of communication. Culture change with an engaged staff will lead to great service and sales. Follow this guide and author your own book. If you believe it, you can achieve it.

Thank you.

Summary

"Assembly required" becomes a relevant reminder because it means you need to put all the pieces together in order to enhance company culture. It takes time. Remember to liken the process to building a model airplane, which is extremely difficult without instructions and especially glue. Recall the parallel to assembling a jigsaw puzzle. Find the corners, build the frame, and then fit together to other pieces. It is also likened to the time that my granddaughter was to receive a huge Barbie dollhouse from Santa Claus. Her dad had the task of assembling the dollhouse before morning. He first sorted out all the pieces. There were many, and the task seemed overwhelming. Next, he reviewed the directions and began with the easiest parts. I call it the low-hanging fruit, the parts he could assemble without the instructions. Then he reviewed the instructions and, piece by piece, continued to build. Patiently, he ultimately completed the dollhouse. It was a masterpiece, and true to his expectation, his daughter was thrilled with what she saw on Christmas morning. Success!

To build a successful culture, you need to sort through all the pieces and identify the easiest parts to assemble. Patiently, one by one, fill in the rest. Step back and enjoy the result of your patience. Building a dollhouse and a puzzle can be likened to building your company culture. It takes time, patience, determination, and working smart. When completed, you have a masterpiece to enjoy, not to mention the pride of achievement.

To summarize the culture improvement journey from 2.8 to 4.5, you need to embrace three components:

1. Self-improvement: You need to be the best you can be. You will be in the spotlight, and the behavior of your associates will reflect your behavior and you. If you are not in a leadership position, then become self-aware of your behavior. Generally you will find yourself reflecting the behavior of your leader. If your leader does not provide the example that has been discussed in this publication, be bold and start practicing the basics yourself.
2. Relationship between you and the individual staff members: You will need to know who they are and what they do. Know their families and friends. Understand their values. Develop them by setting a good example and guiding them in the art of decision making. Be accessible, and talk to them on their level. Encourage them to learn from their mistakes. Be a good listener.
3. Don't be overwhelmed by all the recommendations. You are encouraged to embrace the easiest concepts and build upon them. Please be patient. Evaluate your day, yourself, and your progress. Strive to be better tomorrow, and in time you will experience the ultimate in fulfillment.

I have shared several of my successes, problems, and opportunities in an effort to inspire your imagination so you may now have a guide to help you build a positive culture and write your own book.

www.ingramcontent.com/pod-product-compliance
Lightning Source LLC
Chambersburg PA
CBHW021911170526
45157CB00005B/2039